To: _____
_____
From: _____
_____

Preface

Lord Vishnu, the Creator, the Preserver and the Destroyer, is considered to be the Supreme Deity in Hindu pantheism. He is attributed with a thousand names, a thousand faces, a thousand hands—His names and forms are endless. Each name is significant to His devotees.

Following the world tradition of celebrating the Holy Names of God, we have chosen 108 names, significant of the 108 beads in a rosary which is used during prayer.

The chanting of God's name evokes in us a religious fervour, and helps us to focus on the Almighty.

Vijaya Kumar

Preface

Aditya

आदित्य

Child Of The Infinite

Aditi means 'no limit'. Aditi is the Divine Mother who loves without any limit. God is the mother of all, and like Him, learn to love everybody without limit.

卐 卐 卐 卐 卐

Amaraprabhu

अमरप्रभु
The Master Of The Celestials

The Almighty Vishnu, the Eternal, is Lord of the Gods. He is the womb of the cosmos in whom dwell the gods. He is the Supreme Lord, second to none.

Amritaya

अमृताय

The Immortal

Lord Vishnu, the Nectar of immortality, resides in each of us. This Self in us is immortal. The relationship between the Self in one and the same Self in others is spiritual. Discovering this relationship is entering immortality and becoming aware of the Lord.

卐 卐 卐 卐 卐

Amritasha

अमृताशा

Who Enjoys The Nectar Of Immortality

The nectar that was churned from the cosmic ocean when time began is enjoyed by the gods that makes them immortal. But it is Lord Vishnu who is the Lord of the immortals.

Amrityu

अमृत्यु
One Without Death

Lord Vishnu is the cosmic sound, without beginning or end. He is the Lord who was never born, and the One without death. He is immortal, eternally fixed, and He sees all.

卐 卐 卐 卐 卐

Amurti

अमूर्ति
One Who Has No Form

Our real Self is without form, shapeless, not material. But devotees see God in various forms. He is above all distinctions of form.

卐 卐 卐 卐 卐

Anandi

आनन्दि

Bringer Of Joy

Vishnu, the embodiment of love and happiness, is the manifestation of bliss. He dwells in each of us and brings joy to us. To be aware of Him is to know joy.

Anant

अनन्त

He Who Is Endless

Lord Vishnu, the Eternal, is endless.
He is the Sun and His soul cannot be
measured. He is beyond the knowing
of the senses. His essence can never
be measured. He is diffused endlessly
in all directions, yet He stands still.

Anantajeet

अनन्तजीत

The Victor Of Infinity

Lord of the past, present and future, Lord Vishnu is both victory and victor. He is widely praised and slays the enemies of the gods. He is the unvanquished, and He is eternal.

卐 卐 卐 卐 卐

Anantaraj

अनन्तराज

He Who Has Infinite Forms

Endless are Lord Vishnu's forms, endless His beauty. His heads are a multitude and He is the Self in all. His eyes and feet cannot be numbered. Many and mighty are His forms, but He is hidden.

卐 卐 卐 卐 卐

Anila

अनिला
Ever Awake

Lord Vishnu, the Omnipresent, is never careless and never leaves his post. He gives sleep though He is ever awake and alert. He is the Watchman who never sleeps, but keeps a watch on His devotees.

卐 卐 卐 卐 卐

Aparajit

अपराजित

The Unconquered

The invincible Lord Vishnu is the Origin and the Power. He is supreme and cannot be conquered. He resides in all of us, and we have to discover this Self within us to merge unto Him.

卐 卐 卐 卐 卐

Aprameya

अप्रमेया
The Immeasurable

The Almight Lord Vishnu is without measure or count. He is limitless. His essence can never be measured. He is everywhere, in all directions, beyond one's senses.

Aravindaksha

अरविन्दाक्षा
Lotus-Eyed

Lord Vishnu once takes the incarnation of Krishna. Lord Krishna's beautiful eyes are compared to the delicate, graceful petals of the lotus, signifying tenderness and love.

卐 卐 卐 卐 卐

Atmavan

आत्मवान्
The Knower Of Self

The Lord is the being and essence of all things. He is Spirit, He is the witness and knows all. He is pure and the Supreme Self in all beings.

ॐ ॐ ॐ ॐ ॐ

Avyayah

अव्यायह

The Imperishable

God Almighty, who has no beginning
and no end, is the Eternal One. He
cannot be vanquished, he is All in
all; he is the Lord of lords, the Eternal.

卐 卐 卐 卐 卐

Bhagavan

भगवान
Full Of Glory

Lord Vishnu personifies splendour.
He is full of glory, and listening to His
glory, brings grace. He gives fortune,
and is the Lord of glory.

Bhavana

भावना

Being

Pure existence resides in the being. Lord Vishnu is the Being and Self in every creature. One has to recognise and be aware of this pure Existence, the Self, in order to unite with Him.

Bhutakrit

भूताकृत
Maker Of All Beings

The Good Lord Vishnu is the Creator and Supporter of the physical world, our earth, our universe and the cosmos. He is the One from which creation flows.

卐 卐 卐 卐 卐

Bhutatma

भूतात्मा

The Self In Every Creature

The Lord is present within us as a divine spark that binds us to Him. Deep meditation leads us to the discovery of the Self within us, and the Lord is revealed in every other being as well.

卐 卐 卐 卐 卐

Brahmakrit

ब्रह्माकृत
Maker Of Reality

Vishnu, the Creator and Sustainer, gave us life. We have to respect all life in order to expand our consciousness. Sincere meditation and seeking the real Self is the sure way to God-realisation.

Brahman

ब्रह्मण

The Supreme Godhead

Lord Vishnu, the Being and Essence of all beings, is the Lord of the gods, the Lord of the immortals. He is the supreme Godhead, and he is second to none.

卐 卐 卐 卐 卐

Brahmavid

ब्रह्मविद

Knower Of Reality

The Lord is the Knower of the
supreme reality. The Self, the knower
of wisdom, is pure consciousness.
Seek this, sacrificing your self-will,
and you hear the eternal wisdom
which is the Self.

Bhaktavatsala

भक्तवत्सल
Lover Of His Devotees

The Lord, the Creator, gave life to us. He is the Guru and the best of spiritual teachers. He is truth and His devotees adore Him.

Chakri

चक्री

Holder Of The Wheel Of Cosmos

The Lord has the whole world in His hands, symbolised by the *chakra* (wheel), perfectly balanced on one finger of His right hand. Everything in the universe is held together in this bond of unity.

卐 卐 卐 卐 卐

Chaturbhuja

चतुर्भुज
The Four-Armed Vishnu

Four are Lord Vishnu's form, four His arms, four His manifestations, and four His paths, four are His selves, four His states of consciousness. He knows the four Vedas and reduces them to one word.

Deva

देवा

The Shining One

Lord Vishnu, also called Deva, personifies truth. He is the shining Spirit, shining like the sun. He radiates light and shines in splendour.

卐 卐 卐 卐 卐

Devesha

देवेशा
Lord Of All Deities

Lord Vishnu is the Lord of the gods.
He is the unborn who rules all. He is
the First among the gods, the
Supreme Lord, the support of the
gods and their elder.

卐 卐 卐 卐 卐

Dhanya

धान्य

Giver Of Wealth

The Good Lord bestows wealth on us. He is the highest wealth and is supreme. He is kind and generous and gives a bounty. His wealth is limitless and He gives in plenty.

卐 卐 卐 卐 卐

Dharanidhar

धरणीधर

Supporter Of The Earth

Lord Vishnu is the maker and
supporter of all that is. He carries and
supports this vast earth. He is the
Lord of the fertile earth.

卐 卐 卐 卐 卐

Dharma

धर्म

The Eternal Law

Everything follows the basic fundamental law—that all of existence is one whole. And Vishnu, as Dharma, is the eternal law which the complex universe follows. This universal law holds all life together in unity.

卐 卐 卐 卐 卐

Dhata

धाता
The Carrier Of All

Lord Vishnu is the ordainer and the bestower. He carries the burden of the earth and is the home of all things beautiful. He carries our burden and responds to our prayers.

卐 卐 卐 卐 卐

Disha

दिशा

Showing The Right Direction

Lord Vishnu, Lord of the world, is without arms or legs, He is formless. His limbs are the Vedas. He is a poet and knower of the Veda. Like the Veda, He directs our life in the right direction.

卐 卐 卐 卐 卐

Eka

एक
The One

Lord Vishnu, Who is all, Who is Being and the Essence of all beings, Who is without competition, is the Lord Supreme. He is the radiant One, the unborn, the deathless, the unvanquished, the eternal.

Gadadhara

गदाधरा

Wielder Of The Mace

Lord Vishnu, the all pervasive, is the Law-giver and He is the law. He rules us from within. He wields a heavy mace which is ever ready to end the afflictions caused by physical, celestial and mental afflictions.

卐 卐 卐 卐 卐

Gnaneshwar

ज्ञानेश्वर
Lord Of All Beings

Lord Vishnu is existence, its cause and its support. He is all. He is One from which all creation flows. He is the Lord of all beings. He is the Creator. He supports the breath of life and is the life-giving force.

卐 卐 卐 卐 卐

Govinda

गोविन्दा
The Cowherd Boy

Lord Krishna, an incarnation of Lord Vishnu, is the cowherd, Govinda, of Vrindavana. The tinkling sound of his dulcet anklets is the music of the universe, the garland of fresh flowers round his neck, and the haunting melodies of his flute endear him to the human soul.

卐 卐 卐 卐 卐

Guru

गुरु
Spiritual Teacher

The Spiritual Teacher, Lord Vishnu, is in all of us—our deepest Self. He is the highest form of love, who inspires His devotees to merge unto Him. He is the sacred text and a knower of the Veda. He is the chosen ideal of the learned.

卐 卐 卐 卐 卐

Guruttam

गुरुत्तम्
The Greatest Teacher

Lord Vishnu, the Divine Teacher, is a poet and a knower of the Veda. He is the greatest Teacher who helps us endure the storms of life and unify our consciousness. He knows the sacred wisdom and is the Holy Name.

卐 卐 卐 卐 卐

Hari

हरि

The Thief

The Good Lord, the cause of all attraction, steals our heart with His gracious name. He brings the wandering souls back into His fold. His great brilliance and magnetic forms attract His devotees to Him.

卐 卐 卐 卐 卐

Ishana

ईशाना

The Controller Of All Spirits

Lord Vishnu, holding the cosmos on one finger, is the Essence of all beings. He is the Supreme Law of existence who holds and controls the vast universe in the embrace of unity.

卐 卐 卐 卐 卐

Ishta

इष्टा

Whom We Desire

Lord Vishnu, the chosen Spiritual Leader, is a good friend, giving delight to mortals and immortals. He is One who gives what is desired. Unto Him we should surrender ourselves.

卐 卐 卐 卐 卐

Ishwara

ईश्वरा

The Lord Of All Opulence

Lord Vishnu, the standard and reservoir of vitality, is a vast storehouse of wealth. He is benevolent and His mind is full of wealth. He is the ruler of wealth, and He is the giver of wealth.

卐 卐 卐 卐 卐

Jananah

जनानाह

The Origin Of All Beings

The Good Lord, the Lord of lords, is existence, the cause and the support. He is the Origin and the Power. He is the Lord of the three worlds, the mortals and the immortals. From Him arise all creation.

Janardhan

जनार्धन

The Destroyer Of People's Distress

Lord Vishnu, the Pure and the Supreme, is the ocean of solace in whom we unburden our sorrows. By forgetting our personal sorrows and living for the others, our personal sorrows will be destroyed once and for all.

ॐ ॐ ॐ ॐ ॐ

Jivan

जीवन
Sustainer Of Life

Lord Vishnu has made, and supports, all that is. He rules and gives life. He is Life Itself. He sustains the body and life. He is the preserver of the earth.

卐 卐 卐 卐 卐

Jyeshtha

ज्येष्ठा

The Eldest

The Almighty, Lord Vishnu, whose forms are many, who is everywhere, who is the progenitor of all beings, is the eldest and the best, second to none. He is the Exalled Supreme God, the Omnipresent, Ruler of All.

卐 卐 卐 卐 卐

Jyotish

ज्योतिष
The Supreme Radiance

Lord Vishnu is the brightness of the sun. He is the radiant one, He is enjoyment and enjoyer. He is the sun's rays. Emanating light, He shines forth.

卐 卐 卐 卐 卐

Kamadev

कामदेव

He Who Fulfils All Desires

Lord Vishnu is the Ordainer and the Bestower. He destroys selfish craving and fashions desire. He is desirable and He is desire. He is the Lord who gives what is desired.

卐 卐 卐 卐 卐

Keshava

केशवा

He Who Has Beautiful Hair

Lord Krishna, an incarnation of Vishnu, with his beautiful hair, steals the heart of every being with his attractive form. All creation emanates from the Lord just as hair grows from our body. We are all a part of Him.

Krishna

कृष्ण
He Who Attracts

The name *Krishna* is said to come from the root *krish* meaning 'to attract'. His enchanting smile attracts all things. He is that magnetic force of divinity in each heart, constantly beckoning us to Him.

ॐ ॐ ॐ ॐ ॐ

Lokanath

लोकनाथ
Lord Of The World

The Divine Master of the universe,
Sri Krishna, is the Creator, the Lord
of the earth. As a baby, He allows
his mother to peer into his mouth
where she beholds the entire cosmos.

Madhava

माधवा

The Master Of Goddess Lakshmi

Lord Vishnu, the Supreme Lord, without beginning or end, is the earth and the sky. He is the Lord of Lakshmi, the daughter of the sea. He is the fountain of joy and the salvation of saints.

Mahamaya

महामाया
The Supreme Magician

The Lord weaves a *maya* around us.
We have to seek the Self, and when
the *maya* is removed, we will still be
with the Self, the Magician Himself.
By extinguishing one's self-will, one
can discover that one's Self is the
Lord of Love.

卐 卐 卐 卐 卐

Mahendra

महेन्द्र

Lord Of Lords

As the name signifies, Lord Vishnu is second to none. He is Lord of the gods. He is the seed of all and birth of progeny. He is the Supreme Lord. He is the First among the gods, Lord of the gods, their support.

卐 卐 卐 卐 卐

Maheshvasa

महेष्वासा

Wielder OF The Great Bow

The Great Lord, with his mace, conch and wheel, is also a great archer. He is the warrior, the strongest of the strong.

卐 卐 卐 卐 卐

Manohar

मनोहर

Stealer Of Hearts

He who captivates our hearts is Lord Krishna, an incarnation of Lord Vishnu. The irresistible Krishna who fascinates not only human beings and celestials, but also the cows he herds every day.

ॐ ॐ ॐ ॐ ॐ

Mantram

मंत्रम्
The Holy Name

The Lord is the mantram, the Holy Name. He is the Name behind all names. He dwells in all, so everybody's name is His. Without mantram, life is empty. Seek His love and the emptiness disappears.

ॐ ॐ ॐ ॐ ॐ

Naika

नायका
The Many

This literally means Not One *(na eka)*, meaning many. The Lord is the one reality underlying all of life. His *maya* (illusion) is manifest in his ever-changing varied forms.

Nanda

नन्दा

Source Of All Joy

Lord Vishnu, who has radiance like the sun, is the source of all joy. He is the redeemer of people's distress. To attain the supreme state of joy, we have to see Him in every human being. This vision of the Radiant One will bring forth tremendous joy.

Narayan

नारायण

The Son Of Man

Lord Vishnu is the resting place of all supports, yet He Himself needs no support. He is the home of all and the Lord of all lords.

卐 卐 卐 卐 卐

Padmanabha

पद्मनाभा
The Lotus Navel

Padma is lotus and *nabha* means navel. Lord Vishnu, the symbol of beauty and fertility, is attributed with a navel from whence sprang a delicately beautiful lotus bearing Brahma, the personification of the creative power of the Lord.

卐 卐 卐 卐 卐

Padmi

पद्मि

Bearer Of The Lotus

The fourth hand of Vishnu holds a
lotus which is capable of granting all
rewards or material riches. The Lord
is the bearer of the lotus which is
wealth.

Papanashan

पापनाशन

Destroyer Of Sin

Lord Vishnu, the Creator, the Protector and the Destroyer, is the Lord of all beings. He destroys all sin, all fear, and is a source of delight to all. Every day He offers us an opportunity to veer off from the erring path and seek His protection.

Paramatma

परमात्मा
The Supreme Self

Vishnu, the Supreme Spirit, is the Lord of lord, the One God who is Supreme, who dwells in every one of us, and who is the Essence of each one of us in the universe.

卐 卐 卐 卐 卐

Parameshwar

परमेश्वर
Supreme Lord Almighty

At the core of creation, in the heart of every creature, resides the Lord Almighty. He reigns supreme, the very basis of existence, the Supreme Reality.

卐 卐 卐 卐 卐

Pavan

पावन
The Purifier

Chanting of the Lord's Name purifies the mind. He is a miraculously powerful purifier. He purifies and is the highest blessing.

Pavitram

पवित्रम्
All Purified

Lord Vishnu is the purifier and the Pure Self. He purifies like the wind and He is perfect. He holds strength, majesty and glory, being the Essence of Purity.

卐 卐 卐 卐 卐

Prabhu

प्रभु
The Lord Of All

Lord Vishnu is the universe and pervades all as Lord Vishnu. He is the Lord of all. He is the Lord of all what has been, what will be, and what is.

卐 卐 卐 卐 卐

Prajabhav

प्रजाभाव

The Progenitor Of All Beings

Lord Vishnu is all, the One from which creation flows. He is the Origin and the Power. He is the Being and Essence of all beings.

Prajapati

प्रजापती

The Sustainer Of All Beings

Lord Vishnu, the Maker of all beings, sustains them. He is their true support and the only real source of security. By realising Him, the Self in us, we can truly merge unto Him.

卐 卐 卐 卐 卐

Pran

प्राण

The Energy Of Life

Lord Vishnu is Pran, the life-force in its purest, irreducible form that sustains the body and mind. He is the vital energy and He gives vitality.

Pranada

प्राणदा

The Giver Of Life

The Lord, the Tree of life, rules and gives life. He is life itself. He is self-existent and the Creator. He is the unborn who rules all. He is the totality from which creation flows.

卐 卐 卐 卐 卐

Pratardan

प्रतर्दन

The Destroyer

The Lord destroys the selfishness and
self-will in us that stands between
Him and us, uniting us with Him. In
other words, what was before
creation of cosmos, and what will
remain after its disappearance, is the
Lord, ever changeless.

ॐ ॐ ॐ ॐ ॐ

Purush

पुरुष
Dweller In The Body

The Lord of the universe, the
Supreme Spirit, dwells as a Divine
Spark in each one of us. This Self,
the Pure Spirit, is the same in every
creature that has life, and which can
never die.

卐 卐 卐 卐 卐

Purushottam

पुरुषोत्तम
The Supreme Self

The Great Lord Vishnu is the highest and loftiest Self in the cosmos. By becoming united with the Supreme Person who is our real self, we can attain total fulfilment.

卐 卐 卐 卐 卐

Rakshan

रक्षाण

The Protector

Lord Vishnu, the Progenitor of all beings, is the Protector of all. He slays the enemies of the gods and protects all His devotees.

Rudra

रुद्र

Bringer Of Tears

Rudra is one of Vishnu's names, suggesting tears, Most of us learn of our mistakes only because they bring us sorrow. These tears are a warning that something fundamental in us is wrong and we need to rectify it. The God Almighty warns us through tears.

ॐ ॐ ॐ ॐ ॐ

Sanniwas

सन्निवास
Abode Of The Noble

Lord Vishnu is our home and He is truth. He is the resting place of the ocean. He is the dwelling place of all beings and he gives each a place. He offers shelter and is the dwelling place of the good.

卐 卐 卐 卐 卐

Sarva

सर्व

All In All

Lord Vishnu is the firmly fixed beginning of all beings. He is an inexhaustible treasure. He is existence, the cause and the support. He is the origin and the power, the Almighty Lord.

卐 卐 卐 卐 卐

Sarvadarshina

सर्वदर्शिना

The All-Seeing

The Lord is the all-seeing eternal witness. He is the Lord of all He surveys, ever awake and alert. He sees all and knows all—He is the highest wisdom.

卐 卐 卐 卐 卐

Sarvagnya

सर्वज्ञा

The All-Knowing

The Lord knows all fields of knowledge. He is within us, our real Self, and knows all. He is immutable and the Beacon of all knowledge.

卐 卐 卐 卐 卐

Shantida

शान्तिदा

Giver Of Peace

Deprived of peace, we seek it from the Good Lord who is the giver of peace, happiness and wisdom. He is self-existent and bestows eternal peace.

ॐ ॐ ॐ ॐ ॐ

Sharanam

शरणम्
The Shelter Of All

The Great Lord is the refuge, the
shelter and dwelling place of all living
beings. He is the house of all, the
shelter for the good. He is the womb
of the cosmos from where creation
emanates.

Sharva

शर्व

Destroyer Of Evil

Lord Vishnu, the destroyer of all evil, is armed with an arrow which causes destruction of everything vile. We have to likewise shoot down our self-will to realise our Self within us.

卐 卐 卐 卐 卐

Shashvata

शाश्वता

The Eternal

Lord Vishnu is self-existent, without beginning or end, and perishes not. He is immortal, eternally fixed, He changes not, He is unvanquished, the unborn, the deathless.

Shatrughna

शत्रुघ्न

The Slayer Of The Enemies

Lord Vishnu, the vanquisher of the enemies, has slain the demon Madhu. He is a healer and a slayer of the evil, slaying the wicked and demons in a trice.

Shokanashana

शोकनाशना

Destroyer Of Evil

Lord Vishnu is the destroyer of all that
is evil. Man has to keep fighting
against his self-will in order to merge
with the One. And the Lord will help
destroy this evil if man will but make
the effort.

Shuchi

शुचि

The Purifier

Lord Vishnu is Truth, the Soul of
equanimity. He is the purifier, the
Supreme Self in all, the jewel in the
lotus of the heart.

卐 卐 卐 卐 卐

Skanda

स्कन्दा
Lord Of War

Lord Vishnu is the Supreme Commander who can lead us to release ourselves from self-centredness. He commands the forces of lights and destroys the forces of evil. He sustains as the Commander of the gods.

Sukhada

सुखदा

The Bestower Of Happiness

The Good Lord fills us with joy. He is free from sorrow. He gives delight and is the best friend. He captivates the heart and conquers anger. He is joy and gives joy. He is happiness and brings delight to many.

卐 卐 卐 卐 卐

Sundar

सुन्दर
The Beautiful

Lord Vishnu, in the incarnation of
Krishna, is extraordinarily beautiful—
with a shimmering peacock that
signifies spiritual living.

卐 卐 卐 卐 卐

Sumedha

सुमेधा

Having Noble Brilliance

Lord Vishnu is the womb of all and His fame shines brightly. Son of Vasudeva, he sheds great light. He is the light in the sun. He glows with great brilliance and is much worshipped.

Surariha

सुरारिहा
Destroyer Of Evil

The Lord creates and destroys. He destroys evil and brings happiness. He ends sorrow by destroying the wicked foe and burning out his enemies.

ॐ ॐ ॐ ॐ ॐ

Sureshwar

सुरेश्वर
Lord Of The Gods

Lord Vishnu is the firmly fixed beginning of all beings. He is Lord of the gods and He delights them. He is the Supreme Lord, the Omnipresent.

卐 卐 卐 卐 卐

Sutapa

सुतपा
Who Brings Good From Suffering

Lord Vishnu makes us realise our
mistakes by making us suffer. By
learning from our mistakes we can
take the right path to spiritual
awakening. Lord Vishnu is the home
of light and causes the light to be
visible.

꣖ ꣖ ꣖ ꣖ ꣖

Tara

तारा

Who Carries Us Across

The Good Lord carries us across the sea of birth and death. As we stand in the river of battle that is life, threatened on all sides by evil, the Lord offers to ferry us across to the shore of love and joy. He is the bridge between worlds. He is the safe passage.

卐 卐 卐 卐 卐

Trilokesh

त्रिलोकेश

Lord Of The Three Realms

Lord of the past, present and future, Lord Vishnu is the Lord of the three worlds. He is the earth, the sky, the heaven. In all the three worlds, He is the last resort.

卐 卐 卐 卐 卐

Uttaran

उत्तराण

The Uplifter

The Almighty God alone has the
strength to lift us out of a morass,
out of trouble and despair, and
eventually out of the cycle of birth
and death.

卐 卐 卐 卐 卐

Varada

वरदा

Answerer Of Prayers

Lord Vishnu always appears in answer to an earnest prayer to grant a boon. Every ardent wish is a prayer. He grants and is the means to the ultimate goal.

卐 卐 卐 卐 卐

Varun

वरुण

The Lawgiver

Lord Vishnu is the embodiment of
purity and order in every sphere of
life. He oversees the worlds, the gods,
and *dharma*, and the laws of
righteousness governing the mind.
He makes and protects the eternal
law of *dharma*.

Vasumana

वसुमना
Large-Hearted

Lord Vishnu, the wealth of limitless love, is the God of love and gratifies desire. He is joy and brings joy. He is benevolent and his mind is full of wealth.

Vidvatma

विद्वात्मा

The Most Learned Scholar

The Good Lord knows all fields of knowledge. He is wise and skilful. He is the sacred text and knows the sacred wisdom. He is the ocean of eternal wisdom. He is the chosen ideal of the learned

Vishvakarma

विश्वकर्मा

Maker Of All Things

The Lord Supreme is the Creator, the universal Builder, the divine Master Craftsman who has designed the cosmos. He is the Lord of all beings.

Vishvam

विश्वम्

He Who Is Everything

Vishnu, the Creator, the Preserver and the Destroyer, is the cause of the happening of the world. He is the universe. He who is eternal is the very basis of existence. He pervades all as Lord Vishnu.

Vishvatma

विश्वात्मा

The Self In All

The Almighty Lord is the Spirit who resides in all of us. By detaching from self-will and self-centredness, we can attain unity with the Lord.

Vriksha

वृक्ष
The Tree Of Life

Lord Vishnu, the Sustainer of life, is the Tree of life under whom we seek shelter. He is the sapling providing us with the vital life-force. He is the dwelling and he gives each of us a place.

Yogesh

योगेश

Lord Of All Yogis

Lord Vishnu is Yogesh, Lord of all yogis. He leads those who know yoga. He rules spirit and matter. All yoga has come forth from Him. He is the Master Yoga.

Notes

Notes

Notes

Notes